For Nana and Grandad
with the children

KINGFISHER BOOKS
Grisewood & Dempsey Inc.
95 Madison Avenue
New York, New York 10016

First American edition 1993
2 4 6 8 10 9 7 5 3 1
Text copyright © Grisewood & Dempsey Ltd. 1989, 1992
Illustrations copyright © Sarah Pooley 1989, 1992

Library of Congress Cataloging-in-Publication Data
Salt, Jane.
My giant word and number book / Jane Salt: illustrated by Sarah
Pooley. – 1st U.S. ed.
p. cm.
Summary: Illustrated scenes presenting children's views of the
world introduce words and numbers.
1. Vocabulary – Juvenile literature. 2. Counting – Juvenile
literature. [1. Vocabulary. 2. Counting.] I. Pooley, Sarah,
ill. II. Title
PE1449.S28346   1993
428.1 – dc20 92-31508 CIP AC

ISBN 1-85697-861-3

Printed in Spain

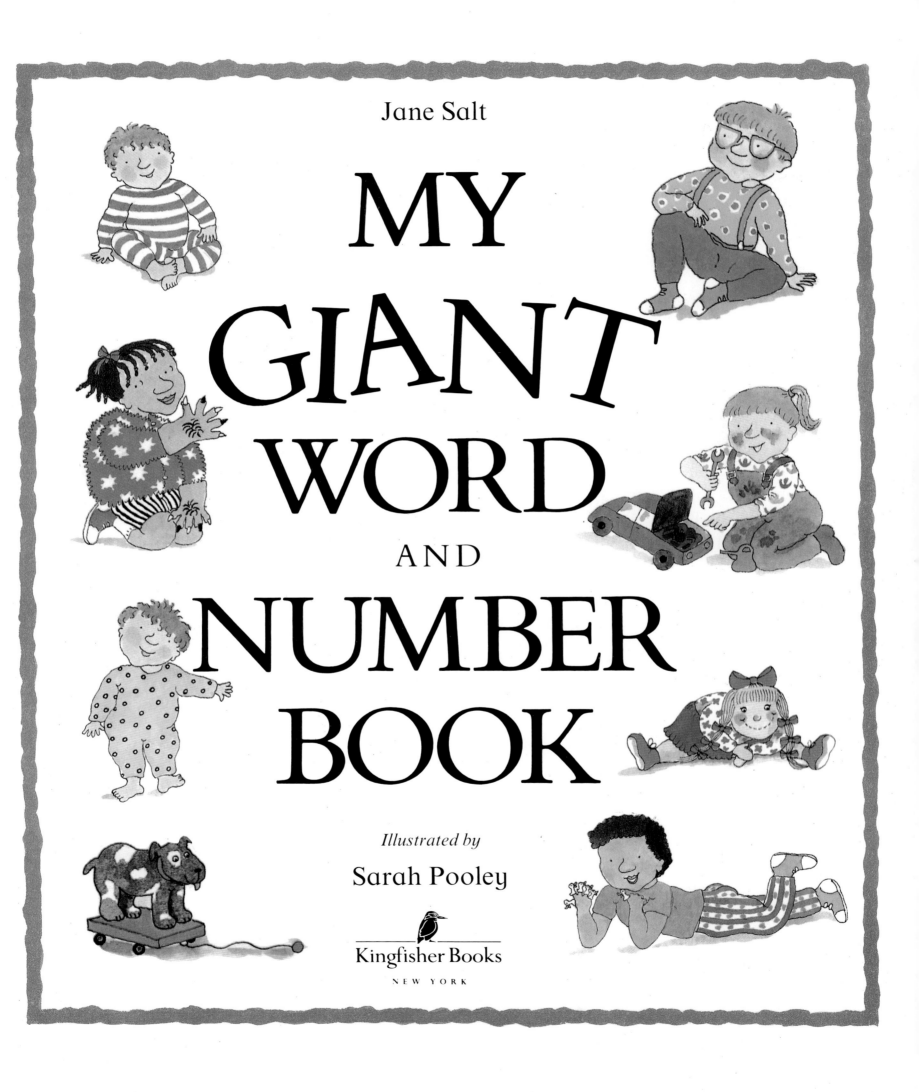

Jane Salt

MY GIANT WORD
AND
NUMBER BOOK

Illustrated by

Sarah Pooley

Kingfisher Books

NEW YORK

Introduction

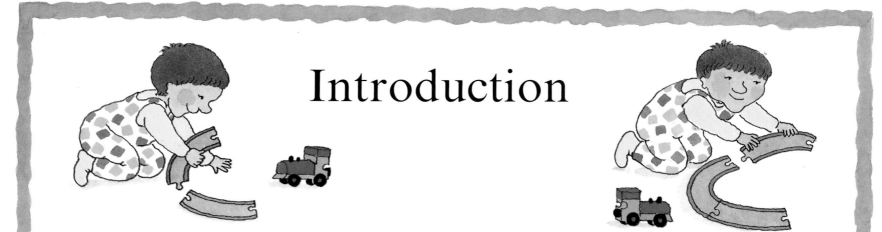

We have designed this book to help you encourage your child's natural curiosity about words and letters, numbers and the world we live in.

Each page has a theme that relates to a young child's own interests and experiences and contains plenty to talk about. Let your child spend as long as he or she likes on each page and take the opportunity as it comes to point out words and count numbers of things. This will help your child to realize how print relates to the words they speak and help to develop an understanding of the concepts of number, shapes, and sizes which they need to expand their mathematical thinking.

Many of the ideas in the book can be extended into games at home. Cleaning up can become a game about sorting into sets. A walk down the street reveals numbers on houses, on cars, and in stores. Make a store at home with cans and packages of food — reading labels and prices is a good way to learn about words and numbers. Above all, this is a book to enjoy together.

Contents

Ryan is one 1

It's Ryan's first birthday.
He's one year old today.

balloons

cousin

Grandpa

Aunt

cat

card

Grandma

present

wrapping paper

ribbon

9

Animal Friends 2

The animals went in two by two,
The elephant and the kangaroo!

panda

kangaroos

horses

dog

lions

leopards

penguin

monkeys

I can't find the other tiger. Can you see it?

seals

elephants

squirrels

rabbit

Noah's Ark

tiger

cats

snakes

ostriches

gorillas

polar bear

hippopotamus

deer

sheep

duck

giraffe

crocodiles

foxes

11

The Checkup 3

Three children have come for their checkup.

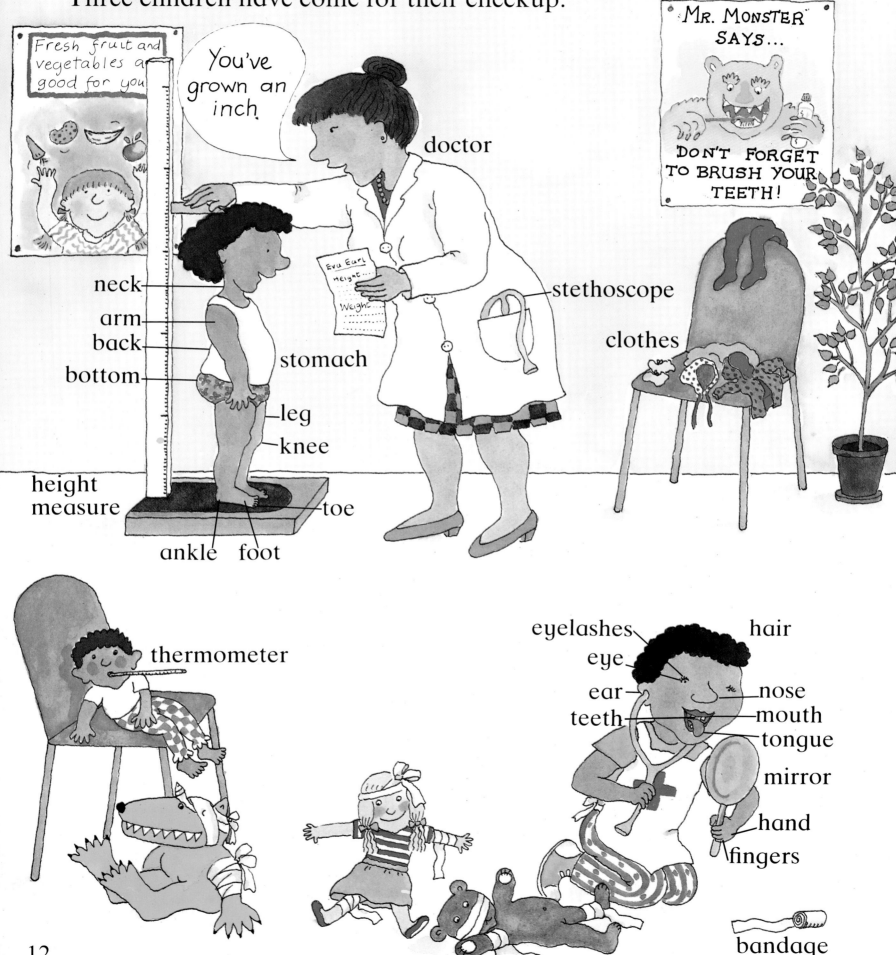

13

Four Kinds of Weather   4

Snowy, windy, sunny, stormy.

snowflakes

skis

sled

snowball

icicle

ice

ice skates

wool hat

coat

mittens

snowman

snow

snowshoes

snowy

hat

wind

kite

cloud

balloon

tree

daffodils

scarf

violets

crocuses

primroses

windy

Which kind of weather do you like most?

sunny

stormy

At School 5

Now we're five, we all go to school.

bookcase

book corner

music corner

shakers

parent

drum

felt pens

crayons

funnel

bubbles

beaker

cushion

book

Higher!

pitcher

blocks

16

"My Mommy" by Tina

I love my baby sister by Emily

I am riding my bike Henry

My favorite food is fries by yolanda

home corner

peas in a pod by Anna

Apple tree by Zack

The very hungry Caterpillar

Bernard

sana

grace

In the Countryside

telephone

clay   pens

blocks   books

paint   paper

crayon   felt pens

nature corner

ress-up box

table

teacher

Messy!

chair

apron

paint

wastebasket

17

Teddy's House 6

This house is number 6.
What number house do you live at?
Can you find any more numbers in your street?

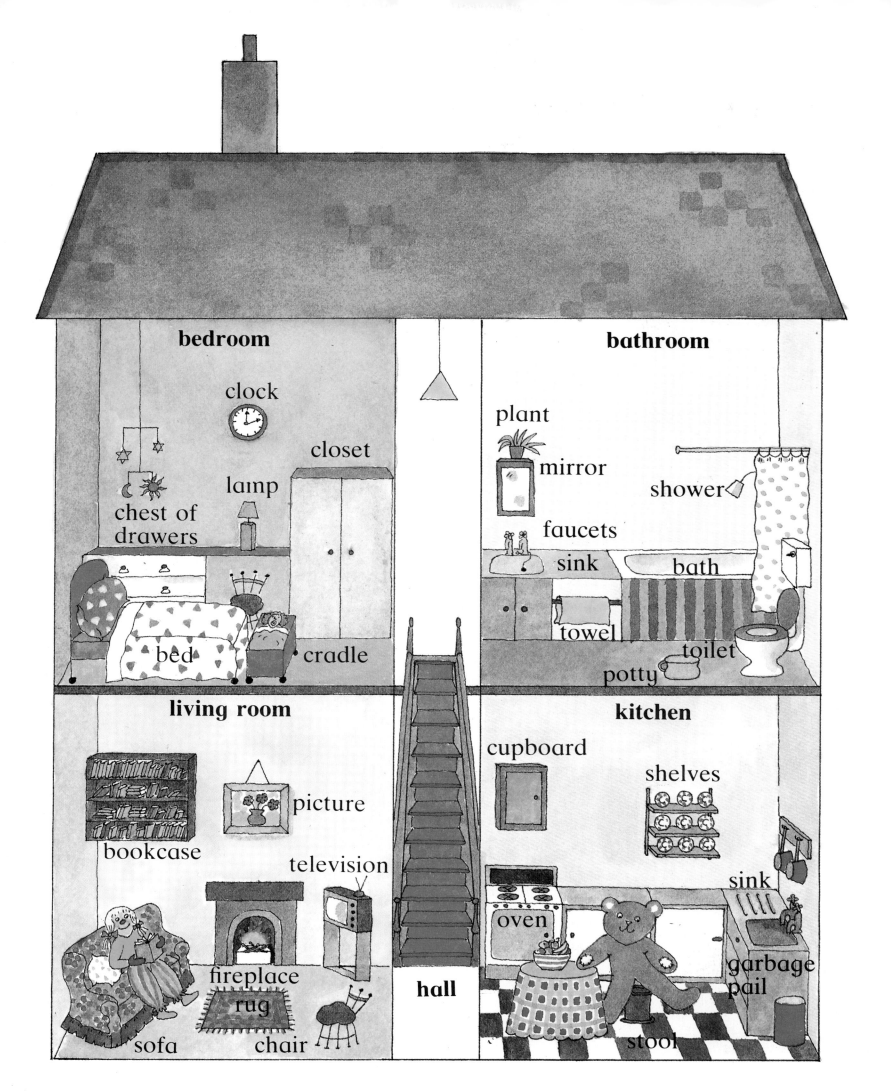

bedroom

clock

closet

lamp

chest of drawers

bed

cradle

bathroom

plant

mirror

shower

faucets

sink

bath

towel

toilet

potty

living room

picture

bookcase

television

fireplace

rug

sofa

chair

hall

kitchen

cupboard

shelves

sink

oven

garbage pail

stool

19

Seven Shapes 7

It is seven o'clock.
Time for bed.

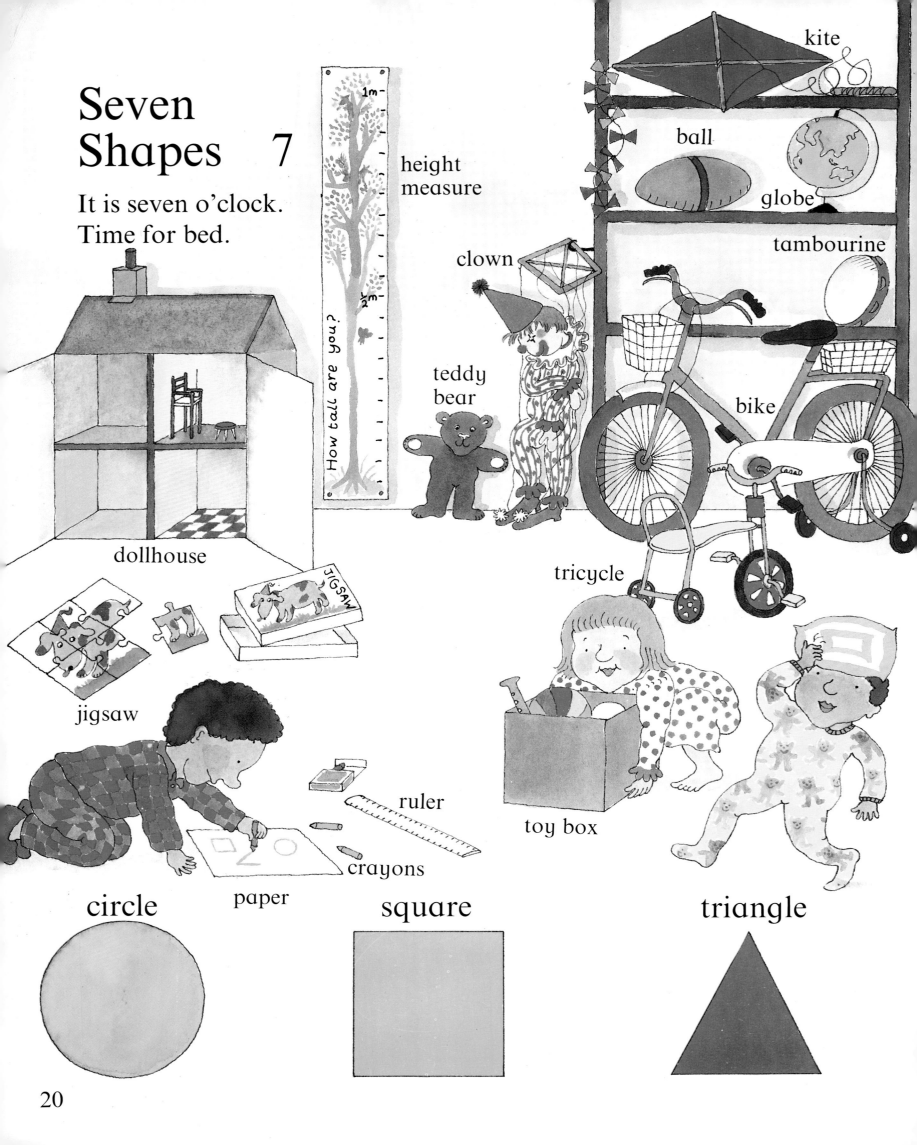

kite

ball

globe

height
measure

How tall are you?

clown

tambourine

teddy
bear

bike

dollhouse

JIGSAW

jigsaw

tricycle

ruler

toy box

crayons

paper

circle

square

triangle

clock

mobile

Humpty

rag doll

pillows

elephant

car

truck

blocks

There are seven shapes and lots of toys.
Can you find more shapes like these in the picture?

rectangle

heart

oval

star

Eight Children on a Picnic   8

How many different kinds of animals can you find?

river

tractor

field

Bridle path

fence

Please shut the gate

Litter

Fresh fruit & veg

tree

bridge

rocks

frog

net

stream

grasshopper

dandelion

leaf

Time for Work 9

We start work at nine o'clock.

Could you type this letter please!

writer

secretary

How many bricks does the builder have?

BUS

Honest Josie's Garage "We'll fix it!"

The big red bus

mechanics

fire engine

helmet

firefighter

hose

ballet dancers

builder

tutu

New Shoes   10

Gloria's feet are size 10.
What size are yours?
You can measure them
here and find out!

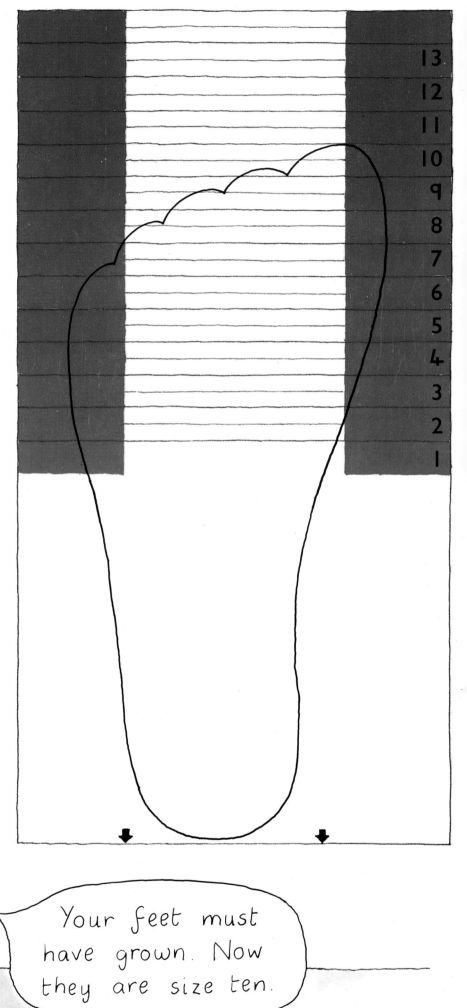

sneakers

They're huge!

boots

Too big.

Oops!

blouse

skirt

Too small.

bow tie

pants

slippers

Too big.

Too small.

That's better!

shoes

socks

These shoes are just right!

T-shirt

shorts

Where does this one go?

dress

Here are the boxes for new boots and shoes.
But which ones go where?

Zero, one, two, three

0   zero

1   one

How many bears have got one ear?
How many bears have hats?
Are there three bears waving?

2

two

3

three

Four, five, six

five

four

Which cars have the biggest wheels?
How many wheels are there?
How many cars don't have roofs?
How many racing cars can you count?

five

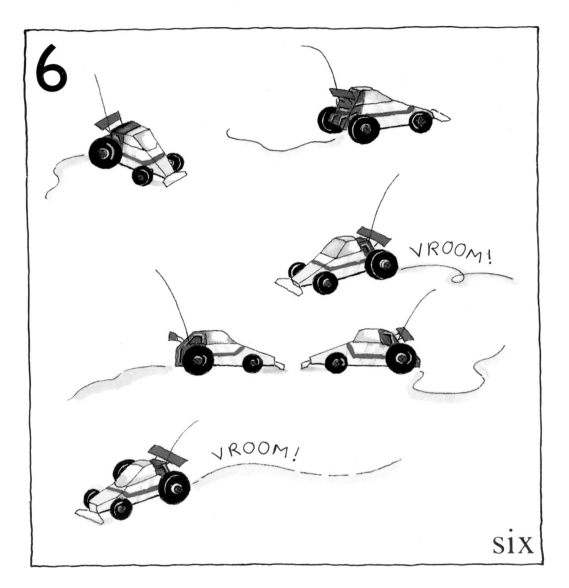

6

VROOM!

VROOM!

six

6 5 4

Seven, eight

7

seven

Are there more baby dolls
or more rag dolls?
Can you count them to find out?

8

eight

8   7

33

Nine, ten

nine

Which robots have robot dogs?
How many are there?
How many arms do the other robots have?

10

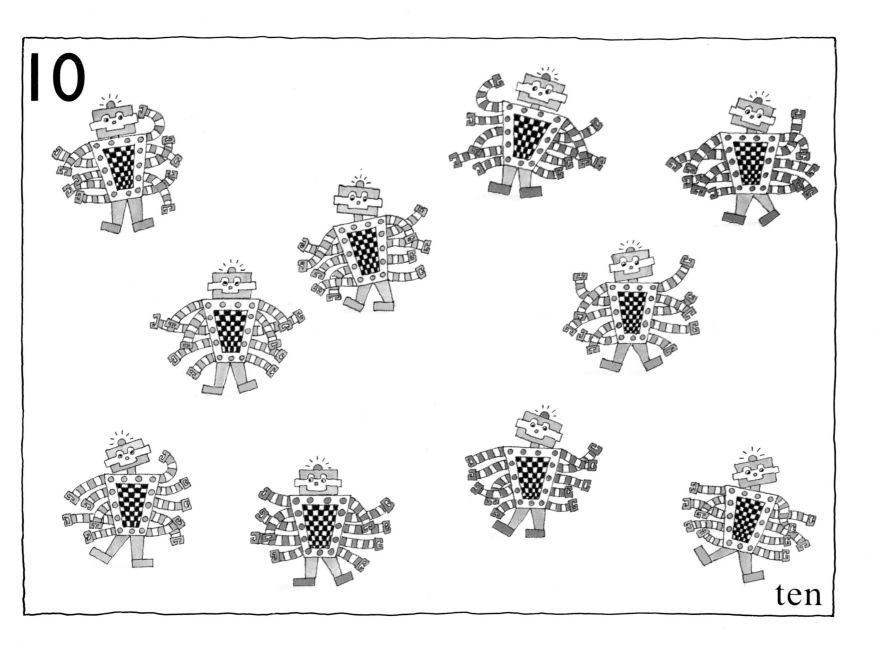

ten

35

Ten Fingers   10

Fingers are very useful for counting up to ten.

One floppy rag doll!   **1**

Two arms and two legs!   **2**

Three!   **3**

Six geese a-laying!   **6**

Seven robot men.   How many robot dogs?   **7**

Look very carefully at the trucks.

Can you find the missing toys?

Ten fingers   **10**

Are there enough?

Is there a hat for everybody?

Are there enough masks for the little monsters?

Can you find the missing shoes?
Which ones are left over?

Help the twins get dressed.
They need matching hats,
socks, and mittens.

39

Building a Tower

David and Natasha are building
a tower. Look what happens each
time they add on one more block.

Two — add on one
more is three.

Three — add on one
more is four.

Four — add on one
more is five.

Five Fat Sausages

Use the fingers on one of your hands to help you sing this song.

43